Johann Sebastian

BACH

Music Giant

Johann Sebastian

BACH

MUSIC GIANT

by Claire Huchet Bishop

illustrated by Russell Hoover

GARRARD PUBLISHING COMPANY
Champaign, Illinois

To

Evelyn and Benjamin Mehlman

in gratitude

for many a beautiful evening

Acknowledgments:

Reprinted by permission of Dr. Arthur Briskier and Carl Fischer, Inc.,
62 Cooper Square, New York, N.Y.:
  Toccata, Adagio, and Fugue in C Major. Copyright © 1969: p. 72 (top)
  Passacaglia and Fugue in C Minor. Copyright © 1959: p. 72 (bottom)
  Great Fantasy and Fugue in G Minor. Copyright © 1957: p. 83 (top)
  "Chaconne" from the Fourth Sonata for Violin Alone. Copyright © 1965: p. 95

Reprinted by permission of Galaxy Music Corporation,
2121 Broadway, New York, N.Y.:
  "Sheep May Safely Graze." Copyright © 1942: p. 83 (bottom)

Reprinted by permission of Edwin F. Kalmus Music Publishers,
154 West 57th Street, New York, N.Y.:
  Prelude in C Major from the *Well Tempered Clavier*: p. 96
  First Prelude from the *Little Clavier Book*: p. 89

Reprinted by permission of Novello and Company, Limited, London:
  Mass in B Minor: p. 121

Picture credits:

Bach: A Pictorial Biography by Werner Neuman (New York: Viking Press, Inc.,
  1961): pp. 46, 105. The document on page 105 is also reproduced by permis-
  sion of the Stadtarchiv Leipzig, DDR.
Bettmann Archive: pp. 1, 8, 59, 68, 77, 109, 112, 126, 139 (both)
Culver Pictures: pp. 2, 117
Bach Collection of Mr. Don Henry, New York: pp. 21, 34
Museum of the City of Erfurt, DDR: p. 56

Contents

1. Uprooted

And now they were orphans. Huddled together in the carriage, the boys could hardly believe what had happened to them. First their mother had died, then shortly afterwards their father too. Johann Sebastian Bach was only ten, Jakob thirteen.

The carriage bumped over the cobblestones of the streets of Eisenach, a town in southern Germany, on a cold winter day in 1695. The boys watched the last houses of their birthplace go by, as the horse trotted on.

"See the Wartburg castle up there, Johann Sebastian?" whispered Jakob. Sebastian nodded. For a short time the boys could still see the

The Bach family home in Eisenach

medieval landmark, high on the hill. Then Johann Sebastian sighed. "It's gone," he said.

With the boys in the carriage was their twenty-four-year-old brother Christoph. He was married and was the organist at Ohrdruf, a town thirteen miles away. He was taking Jakob and Johann Sebastian to live with him.

Although Johann Sebastian and Jakob were relieved to have a home at Christoph's, they were sad to leave Eisenach. Life there had been so gay.

8

Their father, Ambrosius Bach, had been both court musician of the duke who ruled the county and town musician of Eisenach. In those days, princes, dukes, and other noblemen, and also churches, town councils, and religious schools employed professional musicians on a yearly salary. That was the way musicians made a living. Ambrosius Bach played the violin at all the duke's parties, at all the city's festivals and official gatherings, as well as at funerals and weddings.

In Johann Sebastian's home, it was music from morning to night, for his father had to practice for each event. Besides, there was always some musical relative dropping in. The Bachs had been famous as performers for generations.

Bach musicians were scattered throughout southern Germany. Johann Sebastian and Jakob had met many of them, for each year there was a joyous family reunion.

Only last year, it had been Johann Sebastian's parents' turn to welcome the Bach clan. From nearby and far, the Bachs came, each carrying his own musical instrument. They all played and sang together. Between cooking great feasts and looking after the children, the women joined the chorus.

After Johann Sebastian had sung with the others, one of his cousins said, "Now let us hear you on the violin, Sebastian." Willingly, Johann Sebastian played. He had been taught by his father ever since he was a small boy. Cousins, uncles, and aunts had all listened attentively to the youngster.

"Good," they said when he had finished. "You are on your way to becoming a fine musician. What other instruments do you play?"

"The flute, the trumpet . . ."

"And *my* oboe!" put in Jakob. Everybody laughed.

In those happy days at home, young Johann Sebastian used to climb to the organ loft in the Eisenach church, and watch his uncle, the famous organist Johann Christoph, play. This uncle not only played, but also composed church music.

Uncle Christoph had a quick temper, but Johann Sebastian was not afraid of him. He sat quietly in the organ loft, listening to his uncle's new compositions. His favorites were the bold ones that made use of many instruments besides the organ. At that time, church music was elaborate, and some churches had orchestras as well as organs for certain services.

Uncle Christoph let Johann Sebastian watch while he took the organ apart and reconditioned it. Johann Sebastian was fascinated. Soon he was familiar with all the parts of the huge instrument —the keyboard, the pipes, the stops, the foot pedals. "Will you teach me how to play, Uncle Christoph?" he asked.

"Yes, of course."

"When?"

"When you are older and can reach the pedals."

"When will that be?"

"Soon, Johann Sebastian, soon enough."

"I cannot wait!"

"Ah, you are like me—no patience! That's bad, Sebastian. What's the hurry, anyway? We both live here in Eisenach. I can teach you later on."

But now Johann Sebastian was leaving Eisenach and Uncle Christoph, as well as Uncle Christoph's church where he himself had sung in the choir. Johann Sebastian had a clear, soprano voice which pleased people greatly. He loved singing church music, especially the hymns by Martin Luther.

Luther, who had lived at the Wartburg castle in the 1520s, was not only a religious reformer, but also a musician. He believed that the music used in the church then was too difficult for average people to sing. Moreover, the words were in Latin. Luther had gathered the simplest church melodies, as well as many popular tunes and folk songs. Out of these he composed beautiful hymns called *chorales*, with German words.

Johann Sebastian knew many of these chorales by heart. During the church holidays, he joined the other choir boys singing the chorales and folk songs in the streets. People gave the children nuts, apples, sweets, and sometimes pennies. Eisenach prided itself on being a musical town.

Now Johann Sebastian was leaving his choir friends and schoolmates behind. He had studied at the Eisenach school since he was eight. He was so bright that he was soon promoted to his brother's grade. Although Jakob was three years older, he was not jealous; the two boys were fond of each other and liked being together.

Now, bouncing along on the rough road to Ohrdruf, they wondered when they would see their old home again. They glanced up at Johann Christoph. They did not know Christoph well. Did he not look a little stern? What kind of life would they have in his home? What was the school like in Ohrdruf? The orphans' hearts were heavy.

The horse stopped. "Here we are," Christoph announced. Jakob and Johann Sebastian jumped down. On the threshold of the house stood a young woman. She drew the orphans to her and held them tight.

"Poor children," she said gently. Then she added, "Aren't you hungry?"

2. A Mind of His Own

"Jakob! We are going to be together again at school! I am being transferred to your grade!"

"Hurrah!" cried Jakob.

The two brothers were lonesome in Ohrdruf. Christoph and his wife tried their best to take the place of their parents, but the boys still felt lost and sad. To be together at school would make it easier for them to get adjusted to their new life. They had been disappointed when they were put in different grades at first.

The Ohrdruf school was known as one of the best in southern Germany. Yet in no time Johann Sebastian was at the head of the class.

He worked hard in all his subjects—Bible history, catechism, arithmetic, speech, Latin, Greek, a little history, some geography, poetry, including memorizing the Psalms, and of course music, which he liked best.

In those days, most schools were run by the church, and church music was an important part of the curriculum. Soon after their arrival, Christoph had introduced his brothers to the cantor, the director of the choir. "You boys," said the cantor, "will sing in church and receive a small salary. The choir boys also sing in the streets on holidays and divide whatever money they receive then. Ah! I was about to forget—you also get rice and firewood."

Johann Sebastian and Jakob talked the arrangement over later. "Now we can help pay for our upkeep," Johann Sebastian said. "Christoph is not rich, and he has a wife and a baby to support. He needs every penny we can give him."

As professional choir singers and regular school pupils, the boys kept busy from morning to night. When they had some free time, it was spent practicing various instruments: the violin, the oboe, the flute, and the organ. At last Johann Sebastian had grown tall enough to play the organ. Christoph was the church organist, so he was able to teach his brothers.

Christoph also taught the boys to play the two keyboard instruments he had in the house—the clavichord and the harpsichord. Johann Sebastian liked the clavichord's softer sound better. In the clavichord the sound is produced by tiny brass blades hitting the strings. In the harpsichord the sound is produced by quills plucking the strings. The harpsichord has two keyboards and several pedals. Keyboard instruments are often called claviers.

Christoph also began teaching Johann Sebastian how to compose music. The boy learned the rules of music called counterpoint and harmony. He especially loved the kind of counterpoint called *fugue*. One melody is played or sung, then either the same melody or a second one is played as if chasing after the first one. Then a third, and a fourth melody may be added. ("Three Blind Mice" is the simplest kind of fugue.) Johann Sebastian showed an inborn talent for composing fugues.

In harmony lessons he learned how to play

chords and how to combine them. Soon he was able to "harmonize" chorale melodies.

Johann Sebastian had many natural gifts that helped him master music quickly. He had large, well-coordinated hands, a marvelous sense of rhythm, and a flawless ear. Most important, he never tired of learning and practicing. To him it was great fun. Christoph appreciated that, but at the same time he thought his younger brother tried to progress too fast. Johann Sebastian always wanted new compositions to work on.

One day, Johann Sebastian stopped in front of his brother's locked bookcase. Behind the criss-cross lattice work which took the place of glass doors, Christoph kept handwritten music. Johann Sebastian went to his brother.

"Please, Christoph, may I have a look at the music in the bookcase?"

"Not now, Johann Sebastian. In one or two years, when your fingers are better developed."

"One or two years! I cannot wait that long! Please, please, Christoph, let me have it now."

"I said no. That's enough, Johann Sebastian."

Christoph was not mean; he thought he knew

what was best for his brother. Besides, he was strict and wanted Johann Sebastian to be obedient.

Johann Sebastian did not argue, but he had a mind of his own. "I will get that music," he told Jakob.

One clear, moonlit evening Johann Sebastian went to bed as usual in the room he shared with Jakob. He waited until he felt sure that everyone in the household was asleep. Then he got up. Holding his breath and listening anxiously to each creak of the floor, he went down the dark stairway. The living room was lit by the moon. It was very quiet.

Johann Sebastian stood facing the locked bookcase. He put one of his fingers through the crisscross lattice work and, slowly, pushed apart some strips. He worked to make the opening bigger. Then he took a deep breath and listened. Not a sound. His heart pounding, he squeezed two fingers and a thumb through the opening and gently, very gently, pulled the rolled manuscript through the hole.

He unrolled the manuscript and began reading

it. What a treasure! Compositions by master musicians he knew nothing about! He wanted to sit down at the clavichord right then and try the compositions. But he would wake Christoph up. Tomorrow, perhaps he could play when Christoph was out of the house. No, Christoph might discover that he had taken the manuscript.

Yet, he must have that marvelous music! If only he could copy it. Yes, that was the thing to do. He wanted to start copying right away, but the night was nearly spent; he had better hurry back to bed before anyone woke up. With great care he slipped the manuscript back into the bookcase, straightened the grating, and tiptoed upstairs. Jakob had not stirred.

From then on, each moonlit night Johann Sebastian went downstairs and took the manuscript out of the bookcase. Straining his eyes, he copied and copied.

He liked the music that he was copying more and more. Because he was so musical, he could hear in his head how it would sound.

Nights, weeks, and months went by; Johann Sebastian copied and copied. As he copied he learned about composing. Six months went by, and then at long last the night came when Johann Sebastian copied the final bar of the final composition. He had succeeded; the music was his!

Bursting with excitement and pride, he carefully replaced the manuscript in the latticed bookcase for the last time. Clutching his treasure, he made for his room.

Was it his fatigue? Did a cloud suddenly darken the room? Johann Sebastian bumped into a stool, which fell with a loud bang. Then he fell himself, and all the precious sheet music was scattered on the floor. He got up and, terrified, heard footsteps coming down the stairs. He had no time to gather up any papers; Christoph stood in the doorway.

"Johann Sebastian! What are you doing down here? Are you sick? What—what is all this sheet music on the floor?"

He bent, picked up some of the papers, and peered at them. "Johann Sebastian!" he roared. "These are copies of the clavier manuscripts locked in the bookcase! Did you break the lock, you naughty boy?"

"I did not! I did not! I got the manuscript

Young Johann Sebastian copied every note of the
forbidden music by moonlight so that he could play
it on the clavichord.

through the lattice. Please, Christoph, forgive me! I wanted so much to learn these new pieces!"

"Didn't I tell you that you were not to study these pieces now?"

"Yes, but . . ."

"There is no but. You disobeyed. Gather the sheets now and give them to me."

Lips tight, Johann Sebastian handed Christoph his beloved, hard-earned treasure. Christoph took it. "And now, off to bed quickly."

Poor Johann Sebastian! Jakob felt sorry for him when he learned what had happened. Johann Sebastian had lost his treasured music, and now he was about to lose Jakob as well. Jakob was fourteen, and Christoph believed, as their father had, that this was the right age for a boy to become apprenticed to an established town musician. Jakob was to leave Ohrdruf. "I have made arrangements for you, Jakob," said Christoph, "with our father's successor at Eisenach. He is willing to train you."

Johann Sebastian was crestfallen. Since their parents' deaths, he and Jakob had been closer to each other than ever. A little over a year ago, their home had broken up, and they had had to leave everything they knew. Now, Johann Sebastian brooded, separation again. Life is like that: a lot of heartaches. And yet, there was music. And there was God, "a mighty fortress," as Luther had written in a powerful chorale.

When Jakob was gone, Johann Sebastian threw himself into his work at home, at school, and at church. At festival time, the choir boys went about singing together. At night, older students lighted the way with torches, and the *prefect* of the choir, a student–assistant to the cantor, directed the singing. Johann Sebastian became the friend of another singer, an earnest pupil named Georg Erdmann.

Erdmann not only admired Johann Sebastian's beautiful voice, he also enjoyed listening to his friend play on one of the various instruments he studied.

"Make up something, improvise," Erdmann would say. And Johann Sebastian would compose something on the spur of the moment. By then Johann Sebastian knew all the rules of composition, and he used them with imagination.

Christoph was proud of his younger brother, though he remained as strict with him as ever. He never gave him back the clavier music.

By the time Johann Sebastian was fourteen, his brother Christoph had many financial worries. His wife was expecting another baby, and Christoph was not making enough money as an organist to make ends meet. "Johann Sebastian," he said one day, "I am taking on a second job, teaching Latin in the school. We need the money."

Johann Sebastian understood. Though he gave Christoph all his earnings, he had become a burden to the household. He knew only too well what was in Christoph's mind. But Johann Sebastian did not want to be placed as an apprentice to an established town musician. Instead he wanted more education and advanced musical training, not in Ohrdruf, but in a bigger city where more could be learned. How could this be arranged? Where would he get the money to go away?

Luck was with him. One day, Cantor Herda called him and Erdmann. "How would you two boys like to travel a bit? How would you like to go somewhere else to study?"

Johann Sebastian and Erdmann nodded eagerly.

"Well, my old school, at Lüneburg, is looking for good singers. The school is responsible for the music at St. Michael's Church. You will like it there, Johann Sebastian. There is a fine organ and a splendid music library where you will find much that will interest you."

"But, Cantor Herda, I cannot afford any tuition."

"Then you are the right person. The school takes in only boys who are qualified but cannot pay."

"Do you think we can qualify?" asked Georg Erdmann.

"Of course you can. Anyway, you have already been accepted!"

"What?" the boys cried.

"Yes, I have recommended you, and you are expected. By the way, your salary will be higher than here, for Lüneburg is a rich city. Later, you will be able to say, 'I studied at Lüneburg.' Real prestige, my boys!"

"When do we leave?" Johann Sebastian asked.

"As soon as you can get ready."

3. A Big Scare
and a Pleasant Discovery

How cold it was on the road that early morning in March! Johann Sebastian and Georg
Erdmann walked briskly to keep warm. Each
boy carried his few belongings in a bundle. In
addition, Georg carried his flute in a leather bag
and Johann Sebastian his violin in a case.

They had about 180 miles to go, on foot, and
practically no money in their pockets.

"How long do you think it is going to take
us?" Georg asked.

"Ten days, probably. Our first stop today will
be . . ."

"Eisenach! We can visit Jakob!"

"How did you guess? Come on, Georg, let us
hurry."

Soon the Wartburg castle loomed on the horizon, and there was Eisenach. Johann Sebastian was almost running through the streets he knew so well. The court musician who had taken his father's place would be living in the house which had been Johann Sebastian's home. There it was, with its small garden enclosed on one side with a hedge of boxwood, and on the other with a wall covered with creeping vine.

Johann Sebastian knocked, opened the door, and stepped into the hall. A door opened, and a head stuck out.

"Jakob!"

"Johann Sebastian!"

The two boys fell into each other's arms. "What are you doing here?" "Where are you going?" "Do you remember when we . . . ?" It was as if they could never stop talking.

Finally Georg spoke up. "Listen, you two, Johann Sebastian and I have to cover ten more miles today. We'd better get started."

"I'll go with you a bit," Jakob told his brother.

The three started out together. At the entrance of the town the brothers parted.

Johann Sebastian tramped on with Erdmann, his heart heavy.

"Let us sing," Georg suggested. The boys' voices rose in the crisp country air. Later they stopped to rest beside the road and ate their lunch: bread, sausage, cheese, and cake. They quenched their thirst at a spring. Again the two boys were on their way.

As the evening drew near, Johann Sebastian said to Georg, "Let's see what we can do to earn bed and board for the night."

At the next village, Johann Sebastian unpacked his violin and started to play. Georg joined him with his flute. People opened their windows and soon came out of their houses and gathered around the boys.

Suddenly someone shouted, "A dance tune, boys! A dance!" Johann Sebastian struck up a lively, popular Thuringia melody, and everybody stepped about gaily.

Now there was no problem about where the boys would dine and spend the night; everybody wanted to offer them hospitality.

Next day, the two travelers were up at dawn.

The villagers gave them a lunch to take with them, together with good wishes for a safe journey.

Thus Johann Sebastian and Georg trudged along, day after day, rain or shine, singing and playing at each stop for shelter and supper. Sometimes bad weather detained them, but not for long; spring was in the air when they arrived at Lüneburg.

Lüneburg was surrounded by a large protective wall. The boys went through the gate and were awed—this was a city bigger than any they had ever seen.

"Please, sir, where is St. Michael's School?" they asked a man in the street.

"Over there. See that red brick tower, topped with smaller copper towers, rather like lanterns? It used to be an old convent building. Now it's St. Michael's School."

When Johann Sebastian and Georg arrived at the school, they thought it looked rather grim. Rector Büsche, the headmaster who received them, looked rather grim too. The boys could see right away that he would be strict and demanding.

However, that did not worry them; they meant to work hard and to make the most of what the school had to offer.

Soon they were absorbed in their studies: rhetoric, logic, Latin, Greek, French, and theology. Johann Sebastian was doing well in all subjects, particularly in theology which he liked very much. He was pleased to be studying French, for at that time it was the fashion for the German noblemen to speak French at their courts. As these rich Germans were the patrons of music, it was important for a musician to be able to speak French. Johann Sebastian also learned to dance and to fence.

Above all, there was music! In the library, Johann Sebastian was proud to discover some compositions by his uncle Christoph and great-uncle Heinrich. Choir boys were required to study them together with the works of other famous German and foreign composers. In no time, Johann Sebastian felt very much at home in Lüneburg, and he was popular with teachers and students alike. Most of them had already heard of the Bach clan's musical ability.

Lüneburg offered all sorts of opportunities to the teenage boys. At St. John's Church, the organist was Georg Böhm. Thirty-nine-year-old Böhm was very friendly. He did not mind when young Johann Sebastian sat near the organ and listened to him rehearse the music he was going to play the next Sunday. Böhm's compositions were lively, full of sharp contrasts, imagination, and fantasy. Sometimes he would ask, "Johann Sebastian, how do you like this passage? Listen. It's in the classic Italian style. And this has the lightness of the French. This is grave and serene like South German music, your country. Now here is a bit of North German poetic feeling."

Johann Sebastian beamed with happiness. He was learning a great deal.

"You like the composition? Good. However, you have heard nothing until you hear my old master Reinken in Hamburg. You will have to go there someday, Johann Sebastian."

Fifteen-year-old Johann Sebastian liked the idea of travel, especially for a musical purpose. However, at just that time, something that seemed to endanger his entire career happened.

One day the choir boys were assembled in church for a service. The church was full. As usual, Johann Sebastian had been given a solo part. The choir began to sing, then the director motioned to Johann Sebastian to start his solo. A wonderful, high ringing tone rose in the air, then suddenly it cracked and dropped eight notes lower. Johann Sebastian tried to go on, but, to his horror, his voice went up and down. He could not control it. The choir director looked upset; the other boys giggled. Johann Sebastian cast a frightened glance at his friend Georg Erdmann, standing nearby. Surely he would be dismissed from the school, he thought.

When the service ended, Johann Sebastian had to face Rector Büsche. "What kind of behavior is that?" he roared. "Do you have no respect for the church service?"

"Your Honor," began Johann Sebastian—but he said "Your" on a high pitch and "Honor" on a lower one. He could not help it.

Rector Büsche calmed down at once. "Ah, I see. Your voice is changing. That goes with your age. Too bad. We cannot use you for the choir anymore." This was just what Johann Sebastian had feared! His heart sank.

"However, you are a good violinist. We can keep you in the orchestra. Same salary," barked Rector Büsche. What a relief!

Now that he did not have to sing, Johann Sebastian could give more time not only to the violin but also to other instruments, including the clavichord and the harpsichord and, especially, the organ.

At St. Michael's, Johann Sebastian studied logic, languages, and religion, as well as music.

Johann Sebastian liked his organ lessons best of all, and he wanted to know everything about the construction of the instrument. When Mr. Held, the well-known organ builder, came to repair St. Michael's organ, Johann Sebastian climbed up to the organ loft to watch him work. It reminded Johann Sebastian of his uncle Christoph. He saw how Mr. Held removed the manual keyboard.

"You have to remove the foot pedals too, don't you, Mr. Held?"

"Of course."

"Then you are going to test each pipe?"

"Right."

"*All* the pipes; those for the flute, the oboe, the trumpet, the . . ."

"Yes, yes, young man, all of them."

"Don't you think, Mr. Held, it would be nice to have a pipe for bells, too, in an organ?"

"Bells? That's not done."

"That's just it. There aren't any, but there should be."

Soon the organ held no secrets for Johann Sebastian. In fact, only two years later he was considered an expert on organ building.

Johann Sebastian also enjoyed his fencing and dancing lessons, taught by a lively Frenchman who had been a pupil of the well-known musician and ballet composer Lully. Johann Sebastian and the dancing teacher became friends. Sometimes, after the lessons, the teacher would play some new French compositions for Johann Sebastian.

One day the teacher said, "I can see that you like that new French music. Would you care to come with me and visit the castle of Duke Georg Wilhelm in the town of Celle? You know that I am only a part-time teacher here at the school. I also direct the orchestra at Duke Georg Wilhelm's castle. You could hear a lot of French music there, and you might even meet some French people."

"French people in Germany?"

"Duke Georg Wilhelm married a French woman. They both are great music lovers. Come with me at vacation time if you wish. I can introduce you as a visiting member of my orchestra."

The day came when the dancing teacher and his pupil set out for Celle. Johann Sebastian's heart beat fast as they approached the castle. Would he know how to behave at the duke's court?

"You look fine, Johann Sebastian," said the teacher, eying his pupil with satisfaction. Johann Sebastian was wearing his best vest and breeches; his stockings were pulled tight, and his buckled shoes shone. His sword hung on his left side at the correct angle. He had made a graceful loop with his soft tie, which accentuated the dark shadow of his growing beard. His wig was neatly curled. He was slim, straight, and carried himself with dignity.

Johann Sebastian was well received by everybody at Celle. The duke and the duchess told him they would be pleased to have him come back whenever he wanted. He did, many times. He enjoyed the new French music he heard there, especially that of Couperin the Great. It was delicate, clear, brilliant, and elegant. It was full of clusters of small notes, like embroidery around the big notes. It sounded so well on the clavichord!

However, whenever Johann Sebastian returned to Lüneburg from Celle, he appreciated all the more the sturdier German music.

4. Two Herring Heads

When he was sixteen, Johann Sebastian decided to go to Hamburg during his summer vacation to hear the famous organist Reinken.

"Do you want to come with me, Georg?" Johann Sebastian asked Erdmann.

"I'd like to, but I can't. I was just going to tell you my news: I am leaving St. Michael's School."

"What? Leaving? Where are you going?"

"I am going to the university to study law. I don't have what it takes to be a professional musician."

"I wish I could attend the university too, but I cannot afford it."

"Don't worry. Even without a university education you will be a success, mark my word."

Johann Sebastian missed Georg after his old friend left at the end of the term, but the trip to Hamburg cheered him up. He covered the thirty miles on foot.

Although Johann Sebastian was dazzled by the great city, he wasted no time in going to St. Catherine's Church where the famed Reinken was organist. In rapture the youth listened to the seventy-eight-year-old master play. Reinken's talent was astonishing. He was not only a great organist, he was also an outstanding composer. Johann Sebastian was dazzled by Reinken's improvisations. He was especially moved when he heard Reinken play his monumental composition based on the well-known chorale "By the Waters of Babylon We Sat and Wept."

Summer vacation passed quickly in Hamburg for Johann Sebastian. Soon it was time to return to Lüneburg.

Head brimful with music, Johann Sebastian walked back to Lüneburg. Fall was in the air, and a bitter North Sea wind swept across the moor. Johann Sebastian was cold and hungry. He wished for a bowl of hot soup. Finally, after many miles he was much relieved to see an inn.

Upon entering the courtyard, Johann Sebastian realized that this was an expensive place. He had but a few pennies; to eat there was out of the question. Dejected, he sat down to rest outside the inn. A lot of noise came from the rooms— dishes clanked, people talked, called, laughed, and sang. Everybody seemed to be having a good time. And what wonderful smells came from the kitchen! Johann Sebastian could enjoy those free of charge, but they made him hungrier than ever.

Suddenly he heard a window open and then shut quickly somewhere above him. Before he could look up, two herring heads landed at his feet. The fish looked disgusting, but Johann Sebastian was so hungry—better those herring heads than nothing! He picked one up, wiped it off, and began pulling out the edible bits. His fingers struck something hard. What was that? A gold ducat! Quickly Johann Sebastian picked up the other herring head. Yes! Another gold coin! Johann Sebastian was stunned. It was a fortune—half his yearly salary as a church musician.

Whom should he thank? He did not know. From which window had the herring heads been thrown? From what floor? He could not possibly search through the whole inn. Besides, maybe the generous person did not want to be known.

Johann Sebastian walked eagerly toward the door of the inn. He ordered a full meal, including an excellent roast. After he had paid his bill, he had plenty of money left.

Back in Lüneburg he put the money aside and used it from time to time for further trips to

Hamburg. On each of his visits, he learned more from Reinken's musicianship. He also went to the opera in Hamburg and saw Italian works performed. Thus, gradually he rounded out his musical knowledge.

At St. Michael's School he was considered an excellent student, although no one thought of him as a prodigy. How deeply he yearned to be able to go on and acquire a university education! But it could not be done. When he was seventeen and had completed his studies at St. Michael's, Johann Sebastian had to look for a job.

He wanted to go back south, to the green, hilly, wooded country of his childhood. He heard of an opening for an organist at Sangerhausen, about fifty miles from Eisenach. A competitive examination for the applicants was to be held shortly in the church. Johann Sebastian decided to go to Sangerhausen and take the tests.

5. Mr. Bach

When Johann Sebastian entered the church at Sangerhausen, he made a favorable impression on the board of examiners. After he had bowed to the board, one of the examiners said, "Mr. Bach, here is a chorale melody. Will you please fill in the other voices?"

Bach harmonized the melody. Then one of the examiners played a tune on the organ and said, "Will you please improvise on this theme?"

Finally, he was given the theme of a fugue and told to develop it.

The church board was impressed. "So young and yet so talented! He makes a fine appearance too. He lacks experience, but that will come. Let us recommend that Mr. Bach be hired."

Bach was not surprised; he had a quiet confidence in himself. It came to him as a shock, a few weeks later, when he heard he had not been appointed after all. Upon the recommendation of an influential person, someone older had been chosen.

Fortunately Bach learned that a new organ was being built in the church at Arnstadt. Perhaps the church board there would be looking for an organist. However, the building of the organ was going to take several months, and meanwhile Bach had to earn a living.

He thought of music-loving Duke Johann Ernst, brother of the reigning duke of Saxe-Weimar. In those days, Germany was divided into many small city–states, each with its own ruling family. Eisenach, Bach's childhood home, was in Saxe-Weimar, and Bach remembered that Duke Johann Ernst had a small orchestra at Weimar. Perhaps he needed a violinist. The old organist at the duke's court knew Bach and introduced him to his patron.

The duke was delighted to hire Bach as a violinist for his chamber music orchestra, which gave nightly concerts.

It was pleasant to work for such a kind patron.

The duke was particularly fond of music in the charming and refined Italian style, and Bach was glad to become more familiar with it. Bach also enjoyed meeting outstanding musicians who came to visit and play at the duke's court.

The members of the orchestra were all friendly, and the court organist often asked young Bach to take his place at the organ of the duke's chapel. The duke's two young sons, Johann Ernst and Ernst August, both loved music, especially Johann Ernst, who was seven.

Bach saw that he could live a delightful life at the duke's court for many years, playing and teaching. But he wanted the responsibility of conducting the music in a church and playing a church organ that was all his own.

After he had been at the duke's court for five months, the Arnstadt church organ was finished. Before the builder's bill could be paid, the organ had to be checked and tested by an expert. The church board knew Bach's reputation as an expert on organ building, so they asked him to come and test the new instrument.

When Bach saw the organ he was overjoyed; it

The organ that Bach tested at Arnstadt

had been built by a well-known craftsman. It had two manual keyboards, which was unusual for the time. This made it possible to play a different set of pipes with each hand and also to double the volume of sound.

Bach checked everything carefully. Then he tried the organ in a public recital as was the custom. Everyone was enchanted. "Mr. Bach, would you consider accepting the post of organist?" he was asked. It was just what he had hoped!

On August 14, 1703, eighteen-year-old Bach was officially installed as church organist at Arnstadt. It was an impressive ceremony. The head of the church board read aloud a document outlining his duties.

> . . . Johann Sebastian Bach . . . [you are] to show yourself industrious and reliable in the office, vocation, and practice of art and science that are assigned to you; . . . to appear promptly on Sundays, feast days, and other days of public divine service in the said New Church at the organ entrusted to you; to play the latter as is fitting; . . . not to let anyone have access to it without the fore-knowledge of the Superintendent; and . . . in your daily life, to cultivate the fear of God, sobriety and

love of peace; altogether to avoid bad company and any distraction from your calling, and in general to conduct yourself in all things toward God, High Authority and your superiors, as befits an honor-loving servant and organist . . .

The ceremony over, everyone congratulated Bach. "And, by the way, Mr. Bach," said a member of the board, "you will also, of course, train and direct the schoolboys who sing and play in the church."

Ah, Bach had not foreseen that extra job! But this was no time to say so. Anyway, why complain? He remembered his own childhood days as a choir singer and a violinist in the churches at Ohrdruf and Lüneburg. He and all the boys had worked hard; they had loved to sing and play. To teach and direct the Arnstadt boys should not take too much of his time.

6. Trouble and Joy

Bach's duties as organist were not heavy. On Sunday he played from 8 A.M. to 10 A.M.; on Thursday from 7 A.M. to 9 A.M., and on Monday evenings at prayer time.

He made the most of his free time. He practiced endlessly, and day and night he composed music.

Even when he had company, music was the main topic of conversation. Many of his relatives lived in Arnstadt or around it, and they were all musicians or music lovers. He particularly liked to walk, talk, and make music with one of his cousins, Barbara. Barbara was a year younger than he; she was lovely to look at, sang beautifully, and cared about music.

All would have been well for Bach at Arnstadt had the choir boys behaved. But they were not interested in music; they sang and played merely for money. They came to choir and orchestra practice unprepared. Bach was amazed.

"Why don't you know the compositions you are to play?" Bach asked. "Why didn't you do your homework? I saw you roaming the streets last night and fighting one another. Is that the way to get ready to sing and play on Sunday?"

The boys giggled, played tricks, and punched each other right under Bach's eyes. He became angry and scolded them. The boys guffawed—the young master looked so funny when he was angry!

Bach was in despair. "What can I do to make them love music?" he asked Barbara.

Easter was coming. Bach had to compose a *cantata*. This is a work of religious music that requires voices and several instruments. In Bach's time, the words for a cantata were taken from the Gospels or the Psalms. Musicians seldom bothered to make the music fit the words. Bach did. He felt deeply about what the Bible had to say and composed music accordingly.

The Arnstadt Easter cantata was all about Jesus' death and resurrection and was called "For Thou Wilt Not Leave My Soul in Hell." First the music was slow and majestic like a funeral march. Then came a vigorous, joyful melody with trumpets, clarinets, timpani, violins, and violas—death had been conquered by Jesus.

This dramatic music suited the text, and the boys enjoyed it and sang and played with gusto. Bach was delighted and hopeful. But after Easter, the youngsters were just as unruly as before.

One day, at rehearsal, a young bassoon player, Geyersbach, began to make funny quacking sounds with his instrument. Furious, Bach shouted, "Geyersbach! Your bassoon is an old goat!" Everybody burst out laughing, and that made Geyersbach angry. He resolved to have his revenge.

One dark evening, as Bach was taking his cousin Barbara home, Geyersbach darted from a side street and began to beat Bach with a heavy stick. "My bassoon is an old goat!" he shrieked. "But you are a dirty dog!" Swiftly, Bach drew his sword and in no time Geyersbach's shirt was in shreds. Some boys who were with Geyersbach threw themselves between the fighters. Finally, each party went its way, to Barbara's great relief.

"Aren't you afraid he is going to complain?" she asked.

"Complain? I'd like to see him! He started the fight, didn't he? Anyway, from now on, I am not going to teach Geyersbach and the other stupid boys any instrumental music, just voice. Even that is not in my contract!"

The church board argued with Bach and tried to make him continue teaching the boys instrumental music. He refused. Barbara understood his feeling; however, she could not help thinking that her talented cousin was not easy to manage.

In spite of his difficulties with the choir boys, Bach continued to work hard. He composed a great deal, often late at night and in poor light. He perfected his organ, violin, and clavichord techniques. His large hands were strong, and his nimble, accurate fingers never missed a note.

He began to make use of his thumb more and more. This was an innovation; most people at that time played with four fingers only. The great

French musician, Couperin, had been the first to use the thumb, and Bach developed the new method of playing.

One day, as he was practicing, there was a knock at the door. He opened it. "Jakob!" he cried in joyful astonishment. "What brings you here?"

"I am on my way to Sweden. I have enrolled in King Charles XII's army band as an oboist."

"What? In the army? Oh, Jakob, you might get killed!"

"I hope not! It's risky, of course, but I like to travel and have adventures."

"It's so good to see you, Jakob! We must gather together all our relatives who live nearby and have a Bach clan party!"

All the Bachs came on the day of the party, each with his own instrument. In no time, the instruments were being tuned and the sounds filled the room with gaiety.

"First, we will sing a chorale," Bach said.

"And now," Jakob cried later, "the *quodlibet*!"

Johann Sebastian Bach struck a few chords of a popular air; Jakob came in on his oboe with another melody, and everyone began to sing and play a different tune, just as it pleased him. This was the quodlibet, a Latin word meaning "as it pleases."

Soon there was an incredible medley of sounds, yet the Bachs were so talented that they managed to keep the music harmonious. It was so amusing to hear everyone singing and playing at once that it was hard not to laugh. The person who laughed last was the winner of the musical game. What a good time Bach had! He remembered his childhood when his father had led the quodlibet. If only Jakob could stay a while longer!

The day before Jakob's departure, Johann Sebastian said to him, "I have composed a clavier work for you, Jacob—*Capriccio on the Departure of a Beloved Brother*. Listen."

He sat at the clavichord. "Here we are, all of us, begging you sweetly not to leave." He played. The notes went down slowly, separated by silences like sighs. "You won't change your mind, so we tell you all about the possible dangers awaiting you." Now there were short jumps in the music, like someone gasping for breath. "But

Johann Sebastian Bach as
he appeared in the years
at Arnstadt

you remain unmoved. And now, this is the way
I feel." The music wailed and cried in a gradual
descent. "And we have to bid you farewell.
Hear the post horn of the coach coming for you."

"I will always cherish that capriccio," Jakob
said. "The music is just like you, Johann Sebastian
—you have such depth of feeling; you experience
such sorrow, such grief, yet at the end you always
find serenity and joy again."

At Arnstadt, Bach also composed the famous
Toccata and Fugue in D Minor, which rings
with youthful enthusiasm. This composition is
most often played today on the organ or piano.

Although Bach composed many works for the Arnstadt church and played at all the church services, the church board did not forget that he should also be teaching the boys instrumental music. The board kept reminding him of his obligation. He was annoyed, but would not give in. As they kept insisting, he grew restless. One day he told Barbara, "I am leaving."

"Leaving!" she cried.

"Yes. I am going to Lübeck to hear the great organist Buxtehude. I cannot stand this place."

"I was hoping you would stay here for good," she said softly.

He was silent. In a way he wanted to stay because he had become very fond of Barbara, but he felt he had to get away.

He said briskly, "It won't be for long. I want to hear the Evening Music Concerts that Buxtehude gives before Christmas during the Advent season."

"But what about your contract here?"

"The board has given me a four-week leave. Our cousin Ernst will take my place while I am gone."

He left—and stayed away four months.

7. A Scolding, a Wedding, and a Scandal

Bach entered St. Mary's Church in Lübeck around 5 P.M. on a Sunday, just before the evening concert began. He was dusty and tired; he had walked part of the 230 miles between Arnstadt and Lübeck.

The church was packed. Young Bach leaned against a pillar. Suddenly music poured forth and filled the church. Bach forgot his fatigue. Never before had he heard anything so commanding. The organ was a beautiful instrument, and the organist, Buxtehude himself, was an astonishing performer. The members of the orchestra played extraordinarily well, and the singers were perfectly trained.

This old print of a church concert in the 1700s appeared in a musical dictionary of the period.

Bach was particularly impressed by the beauty of Master Buxtehude's compositions. He delighted in the way Buxtehude introduced fiery fantasy in the usually sedate accompaniment of the chorale. "I'll do the same at Arnstadt!" Bach promised himself.

Arnstadt? How faraway it seemed! Indeed, after but a few days, Arnstadt ceased to exist for the young musician. He attended all the concerts in Lübeck and spent the rest of the days going to rehearsals and listening endlessly to Buxtehude's practicing on the organ. He also probably played on the organ himself in the master's presence.

One day Buxtehude said, "You are very gifted, Mr. Bach, and you appreciate this beautiful instrument. Two years ago I had a visit from another talented young man by the name of Handel. I believe he lives in England now. He, too, liked this organ. I had hoped. . . . Well . . . why don't you come home with me and meet my daughter?"

Bach could not help feeling very happy—obviously Buxtehude had singled him out as his possible successor at this marvelous organ! However, Bach knew the North German custom of the time

—he would have to marry the organist's daughter. Buxtehude himself had had to do this when, as a young man, he had succeeded the former St. Mary's organist.

It turned out that Miss Buxtehude was thirty years old and very far from being attractive. She could not compare to Barbara.

Barbara! Bach had told her last October that he would be gone four weeks. And this was the end of January! In a hurry he took leave of Master Buxtehude and headed for Arnstadt.

He reached Arnstadt on February 21 at the end of the week. Without taking the time to call on the board, he resumed his organist duties that very Sunday.

At that time, at the Sunday service, it was the custom for the organist to "prelude," that is, to improvise before the congregation sang the chorale in order to give the people time to find their places in the hymn book. Bach began to prelude in the brilliant style that Buxtehude had used in Lübeck. The music went on and on. People became fidgety. When Bach at last gave them their cue to sing, their troubles were not over. Each time they held a long note, the organist would introduce a cascade of little grace notes, or even an unexpected variation.

At last the service was over. The church board summoned Bach. He went in with his head high. After all, what was Arnstadt compared with Lübeck where the great Buxtehude himself had singled him out as his possible successor?

"Mr. Bach, you were given a four-week leave and you were away four months. What do you have to say?"

"I went to perfect my art, and the person I left in charge was fully competent, was he not?" Bach answered coldly.

The board chose not to pursue that question, and, instead, dealt with another complaint. "Mr. Bach, we want to warn you that we are very much displeased with the way you introduced these pretentious preludes and variations in the church service. The congregation was confused. We give you a week to think things over and make a definite promise to change your ways."

A silence followed. Bach bowed and went out.

The week passed. Stubborn Bach did not say

a word, and the lenient board did not mention the matter again. But before the end of the year, Bach was called before the board again.

"Mr. Bach, are you or are you not going to teach the choir boys instrumental music? They have become totally unruly. Some play ball in the church during the service. One even left during the office and went to a tavern to drink.

"We have new complaints about your music too. You used to prelude too much before the chorale. Now you have stopped preluding altogether."

Indeed he had. After the first complaint about preluding too long, he had decided not to prelude at all! Impatient and angry, he said, "I will explain it all in writing," and prepared to withdraw grandly.

"We have not finished with you yet, Mr. Bach," said a board member. "There is still a most serious matter to examine. Recently you invited a girl to the organ loft, and you played and sang together. You know very well that women are not allowed in the organ loft, and least of all to make music."

"I secured the minister's permission," Bach

snapped. He was boiling with rage. Now they were complaining about Barbara. This was too much. He could not stand such meddling! Although he had been in Arnstadt four years, he would have to leave.

At about this time the post of organist became vacant in the nearby town of Mülhausen. Bach went to Mülhausen and played for the church board. They were most enthusiastic. After the performance he was offered the same salary as in Arnstadt, plus firewood and free flour and fish.

Back in Arnstadt he told Barbara the good news. "I shall be settled in Mülhausen within three months," he said. Then he added with a mischievous gleam in the eye, "Can you wait that long for our wedding?"

They were married very simply in a country church near Arnstadt. In Mülhausen the organist's living quarters were large enough so that the young couple could take an advanced music student as a boarder. The student helped with Bach's younger day pupils, while studying himself. Martin Schubart, who was seventeen and very gifted, was Bach's first resident pupil.

The twenty-two-year-old Bach was immensely happy. He overflowed with energy and ideas. His first cantata to be heard in Mülhausen, "God Is My King," was composed for the inauguration of the new town council. He gathered together instrumentalists and singers from the town and from the villages around.

This cantata was a splendid work. It had something of Buxtehude's grandeur, but was warmer and less rigid. The council decided to have the cantata printed. This was the only Bach cantata printed during his lifetime, though he composed several hundred. Only 190 are available today; the others were lost.

Most of the Mülhausen people were proud of their organist. However, some of them were not, and among them, unfortunately, was the minister of the church. He fumed at the city council meeting.

"What is the matter with that young organist?" he cried. "Has he no respect for the sanctuary? Does he not know that church music has to be restrained, quiet, dignified? Mr. Bach has introduced shameful fantasy into the house of God.

Believe me, this newfangled music smacks more of the theater than of the church. It is frivolous and worldly. Indeed, it is the devil's work if you ask me, and is a danger for the soul's salvation."

The council was embarrassed. Bach was appalled. He was a devout Christian, a Lutheran. He had never intended any disrespect to the church. He could not understand how music, beautiful music, could serve any purpose other than God's greater glory.

Soon the town became thoroughly divided for and against the daring young organist. By the time Bach had been there a year, he grew tired of the quarrel. "Barbara," he said, "I think that we had better take the first opportunity that comes along and go somewhere else."

8. A Happy Household

"Come here, Friedemann! You cannot have breakfast yet. Dorothea, come to the clavichord too. Papa is ready for the chorale singing."

Five-year-old Dorothea and three-year-old Friedemann hurried to stand by their father, who was seated at the clavichord. Bach struck the chord of a chorale tune, and the entire family began to sing. When singing was over, they all sat down to eat breakfast.

Besides Bach, Barbara, and the two children, the household included Martin Schubart and two young Bach cousins, one of them his brother Christoph's son. Bach felt it was his duty to teach the two cousins free of charge.

A view of the town of Weimar during Bach's time

The Bachs were now living in the town of Weimar. Bach had left Mülhausen in 1708, and was employed by the duke of Saxe-Weimar, Wilhelm Ernst, elder brother of the duke he had worked for earlier. Bach was the court organist and a member of the court orchestra. He hoped to be made *cappellmeister*, director of all the music at the duke's castle someday, since the musician Drese, who held the title, was quite elderly.

Weimar castle, with its chapel spire, rose above the forest outside Weimar. Duke Wilhelm was devoted to both religion and music. He had a court orchestra of about twenty musicians, dressed in uniforms as was the custom. Bach played either the violin or the clavichord, depending on the music. For the court organ Bach invented a set of pipes imitating the sound of bells. He was greatly pleased with this carillon, which he had wanted ever since he was a small boy.

In Weimar, Bach's salary steadily increased. However, he was still very careful with money; he remembered only too well his lean childhood and adolescent years.

Barbara and her husband discussed every household purchase—except musical instruments. On these Bach knew no restraint; soon the house was filled with clavichords, harpsichords, violins, violas, cellos, flutes, and so forth.

Besides his duties at court, Bach gave music lessons to his resident students and to town pupils, including the two sons of Duke Johann Ernst, whom he had met during his first stay at Weimar. The two boys were gifted, especially Johann Ernst, Jr., who composed well. Bach delighted in teaching all these young people; he had no discipline problem with them because they were all eager to learn.

Bach also traveled fairly frequently. He was becoming so well known as an organist and as an expert on organ building that he received many invitations to give concerts and to examine organs.

Duke Wilhelm understood that such an expert would be in demand throughout the countryside. "Go, Mr. Bach," he said whenever his talented employee received an invitation. "Just make sure someone competent takes your place while you are gone." Bach's advanced pupil, Schubart, became his assistant and was able to take over.

Bach enjoyed visiting his many relatives and also his musical friends. One of his good friends was the scholar Johann Matthias Gessner, who admired Bach greatly. Another was the famous composer Georg Philipp Telemann, who was only four years older than Bach. The two men had a wonderful time together, playing and discussing music, and sharing ideas on the construction of musical instruments.

On one of his visits, Bach told his friend, "Philipp, my family has increased. We have another boy. Will you be Carl Philipp Emanuel's godfather?" Telemann accepted gladly.

Another good friend was Georg Walther, who was the Weimar town organist. Walther showed Bach a number of original Italian works he had in his possession. Bach was greatly interested because, so far, he had known Italian music only as it had inspired German composers; he had never heard or seen original Italian scores.

Bach was immediately enthusiastic about the compositions of Frescobaldi, Corelli, and especially Vivaldi. He admired their clarity, gracefulness, and simplicity.

Bach liked Vivaldi so much that he transcribed three of his violin concerti so they could be played on the organ. He also transcribed sixteen string concerti for the clavichord. He was not content to transcribe note for note from one instrument to the other. He used his imagination and gave breadth and strength to the works which, finally, were no longer Vivaldi's but Bach's.

The Italian music inspired him greatly. He never imitated, but he created several splendid new compositions full of feeling and depth, which combined the Latin and the German genius. Among them is the well-known Toccata, Adagio, and Fugue in C Major. Its slow movement, the adagio, is almost unbearable in its incredible beauty.

At this same time he also wrote the charming Little Fugue in G Minor and the triumphant Passacaglia and Fugue in C Minor. The passacaglia was a slow Spanish dance popular at the court of Celle, which Bach had visited. In Spanish, *pasar* means "walk" and *calle* means "street." Bach used a melody by the French composer André Raison, and from this quiet "walk on the street" he created a sublime masterpiece.

Those days in Weimar were full and gay. Christmas 1715 was especially joyful, for Barbara had given birth to another son. Bach composed a lovely work for the church service of the first Sunday after Christmas, "Walk Ahead on the Faith Path." This composition has remained one of his most popular cantatas.

One day, Bach came home in a happy mood. "Barbara," he said, "the duke has made me the orchestra leader."

"Wonderful! You deserve it. One of these days, I am sure you will be made cappellmeister."

Bach's duties still included composing cantatas for the duke's chapel. For the words of many of them, he used poems by his good friend Salomo Franck, the court librarian.

Bach was busy from early morning until late at night, playing, composing, and teaching. One of his favorite pupils was talented eighteen-year-old Prince Johann Ernst.

"I am worried about the prince," Bach told Barbara one day. "He is not well. He has seen several doctors, but no one seems to know what ails him."

During the following months, the prince's health became worse. Finally, Johann Ernst said to Bach, "Master, I shall have to leave Weimar and try to find a cure somewhere else."

Bach was heartbroken. He took one of Franck's poems, "I Had So Much Grief," and composed a farewell cantata. In it, Bach expressed his unshakeable faith in God, despite human suffering and even death. Bach was never to see his beloved pupil again, for he died several months later.

9. A Hunt and a Contest

"Mr. Bach," Duke Wilhelm said one day, "my friend and neighbor, Duke Christian of Weissenfels, is going to celebrate his thirty-fifth birthday with a huge hunting party. After the hunt there will be a dinner. My friend is anxious to have some dinner music. I told him that you and Franck would arrange it. Give us something lively. Franck must not forget to mention Duke Weissenfels himself."

Bach composed graceful music on a rather trivial text by Franck. It began with a song, "What I Delight in Is a Gay Hunt"; it ended praising the glory of the duke of Weissenfels.

It was a great success. Bach himself liked the composition so much that he used it over and over again for other events. It even became the theme of his well-known church cantata "Thus God So Loved the World." Bach drew no line between sacred and secular music—for him there was just music.

When Bach accompanied Duke Wilhelm to parties, or when he went to musical festivities such as the dedication of a new organ, there were often huge dinners. Bach enjoyed delicious food, and on his return home he would delight his children by describing the menu.

"There were a lot of French dishes," he told the children after one banquet. "Fish cooked in vinegar, and beef simmered in red wine and brandy, with onions, carrots, and spices. It was excellent."

"Was that all?" asked Friedemann.

"Certainly not. Then we had smoked ham, a roast quarter of mutton, a veal roast, potatoes, peas, spinach, boiled pumpkin, lettuce, warm asparagus salad, radishes, fresh butter, preserved lemon rind and cherries. And, of course, beer and Rhine wine."

"Did you eat *everything*, papa?" Dorothea asked.

Bach agreed to take part in a musical contest with Louis Marchand (right), a well-known organist and clavier player.

"Yes, everything. After all, how could one by-pass those sweet presents from God!"

Bach enjoyed especially a trip to Dresden in 1717. Volumier, the concert director at the court of August Saxe, king of Poland, invited him to enter an unusual musical contest there.

"My rival will be Louis Marchand," Bach told Barbara when the invitation arrived. "He's the famous French organist and clavier player and is now visiting in Dresden. I am delighted to have an opportunity to hear him. I will take the first post coach."

Volumier received Bach with open arms. "Mr. Bach," he said, "let me explain the situation here. The king has taken a tremendous liking to this Marchand and wants to hire him. I believe the king is making a mistake. Marchand is most unreliable, a very flighty person. I hope that when the king hears you play, his enthusiasm for Marchand will wane."

"Marchand is playing at a nobleman's party today," went on Volumier. "I have arranged for you to hear him in an adjoining room without anyone knowing about it."

Bach listened to Marchand play. Then he wrote him a polite letter saying that he was willing to take part in a contest with him. He was ready to improvise on any theme Marchand would care to give him, and he would expect Marchand to do the same on one of his. Marchand accepted.

On the day of the event, everyone was most excited. Wearing his dark suit, his wig neatly curled, Bach made his way up the marble stairway of Count Fleming's palace, where the contest was to take place. Beautifully dressed men and women hurried to the music room. Servants stood on the steps, holding flaming torches.

"His Majesty the king!" the master of ceremonies loudly announced.

As the king came in, the ladies curtsied and the men bowed low. When the king sat down, Count Fleming came forward, bowed again, and asked to be permitted to introduce Mr. Bach. The king greeted Bach, then, turning to Count Fleming, asked, "And where is Mr. Marchand?"

"He is on his way, Your Majesty," answered Fleming nervously.

"On his way! And *I* am here! Why didn't you send for him earlier?"

"I did, Your Majesty. He will surely be here any moment," said Count Fleming, glancing anxiously at the entrance. "Ah, here he . . ." But it was only the servant Fleming had sent after Marchand.

There was a brief, low conversation. Then, flushed and embarrassed, Count Fleming turned to the king. "Your Majesty, something incredible has happened. Mr. Marchand has left Dresden by

the fast coach. I don't know what to say. I don't understand. I am deeply ashamed, Your Majesty."

"Mr. Marchand left? Well, well . . . too bad. . . . It would have been interesting. . . . But, my dear Fleming, we still have Mr. Bach here! We can decide by ourselves whether or not he is superior to Mr. Marchand. Mr. Bach, show us what you can do."

Bach sat down and began to play. The audience was completely silent, dazzled by his playing. When he stopped, the king said, "Go on, please, Mr. Bach." King August leaned forward in his armchair to see better as Bach continued. When the music finally ended, everybody turned towards the king, waiting for his opinion.

King August said, "Wonderful, wonderful! Unbelievable. Mr. Bach, how did you arrive at such perfection in your art?"

"I worked hard, Your Majesty. That's all. Anyone who works as hard will do as well."

"You are an uncommonly modest man, Mr. Bach. Thus you add virtue to talent. There is no question in my mind between you and Mr. Marchand. You are the better of the two."

The guests broke into applause. Then they surrounded Bach and paid him all sorts of compliments. His performance had been a triumphant success.

That evening, as he was relaxing at the home of Volumier, the concert director, a servant brought him a present from the king. It was a purse with one hundred French gold pieces. As Bach was busy talking with other musicians, the king's servant gave the purse to one of Volumier's servants, who put it on a table. The purse disappeared and was never found.

Bach went back to Weimar covered with glory as a performer of music, but without any money to show for his work.

Although Bach was famous for his technical ability as a performer, few people were aware of his greatness as a composer. At that time all musicians were expected to compose original works as part of their professional duties, so Bach did not seem unusual. Also, many people felt his music was too serious and complex, and preferred the light, sentimental melodies popular at that time.

However, during his years in Weimar, Bach composed some of his most memorable masterpieces. Among them was the G Minor Fantasy and Fugue (the "Great"), with its challenging opening call, a stupendous feeling of space in the fantasy, and sprightly and determined rhythm in the fugue.

Another famous work was a cantata that includes the tender and well-known melody, "Jesus, Joy of Man's Desiring."

Also from this period is the popular "Sheep May Safely Graze."

10. Palace and Prison

All of the musicians who played for Duke Wilhelm were also expected to play at the court of his brother Duke Johann Ernst. When this duke died in 1707, his son, Ernst August, Bach's former pupil, became duke. The new duke was much attached to his old music teacher, and Bach enjoyed playing at his court.

Duke Wilhelm had never gotten along well with his nephew, and when the young man began to reign, their relationship became worse. The young duke was an autocratic ruler; he announced that anyone criticizing his way of governing would be thrown into jail.

"Can you imagine such a thing, Mr. Bach?" fumed Duke Wilhelm. "That nephew of mine, a tyrant! Well, I won't have anything to do with him anymore. And, from now on, I forbid all my musicians to go to his castle and play for him. And that goes for you too, Mr. Bach."

Bach listened to the duke, but did not say anything. For years he had helped develop Ernst August's musical taste and ability. He loved the young man in spite of his tyranny. Bach paid no attention to Duke Wilhelm's command.

Duke Wilhelm was furious. "So that's the way Mr. Bach acts! Well, we will see who has the last word here!"

Soon afterwards, Cappellmeister Drese died. Bach came home from the castle, red with anger. "Barbara! The duke has appointed Drese's son as cappellmeister! Why should I stay here where I am not appreciated? At the first opportunity we will move away!"

Bach went to see Duke Ernst August and his wife, the princess of Anhalt-Cöthen.

"It has become impossible for me to stay in Weimar," Bach told them.

The duke and his wife understood. "Do not worry, Mr. Bach," the princess said. "I shall talk to my brother, Prince Leopold of Anhalt-Cöthen. Maybe he will be able to find another position for you."

Prince Leopold asked Bach to be his cappellmeister, and offered him a much bigger salary than he was earning in Weimar.

Bach accepted. He handed his resignation to Duke Wilhelm, adding that he had arranged for Schubart to replace him.

"What?" cried Duke Wilhelm, outraged. "You are a headstrong, stubborn man, Mr. Bach. You defied my orders and went on making music at my nephew's. And now you want to cancel our contract and have even decided who is to take your place. Well, Mr. Bach, I am not such a fool! I do not accept your resignation. You are to stay with me!"

Bach did not argue; he just stopped composing any new cantatas for the chapel. He cut his duties to the barest minimum, and he bothered everyone with his raging complaints. In no time he made himself impossible, so much so that Duke Wilhelm had him arrested. The court secretary's report read:

On November 6, the orchestra leader and organist Bach was confined to the County Judge's place of detention for too stubbornly forcing the issue of his dismissal.

Bach did not mind being imprisoned. He took advantage of the quiet and wrote the *Little Organ Book* as a first book for his organ pupils.

A month went by. Duke Wilhelm saw that he could not break Bach's will. The court secretary recorded:

On December 2, he [Bach] was freed from arrest with notice of his unfavorable discharge.

Bach did not care about the unfavorable discharge. He was free. He took his family and moved to Prince Leopold's court in Cöthen.

There he recopied his *Little Organ Book* manuscript and had it leather bound. This thin volume has remained to this day the first textbook for all organ pupils. Some of the chorales in the book are particularly well known, such as "Adorn Thyself, O My Soul" and "From the Heights of Heaven I Have Come."

11. Studying with Papa

"Now Friedemann, place your fingers on the keys. Good. Now press the keys down with the tips of your fingers, keeping your hand gently hollowed. Good! Now, play."

Eight-year-old Friedemann, sitting at the clavichord, tried hard to follow his father's directions.

"Do you hear what lovely sounds you make when you play that way, Friedemann? You do not strike the keys; your fingers are constantly in contact with them. Each tone is like a pearl, and all the pearls smooth and equal."

"But, papa, I'm tired of these exercises! Exercises! Exercises! Nothing but exercises! I want to play a real composition."

"You have been working on those exercises for only six months. Most of my pupils do nothing else for a year. Yet, you are bored. . . . Well, I understand. I was once a boy myself, Friede dear. Let me see. . . . Shall I make up a small composition, especially for you? Something like this. Listen!" And on the spur of the moment, Bach improvised a tiny prelude.

"Do you like it, Friedemann? Would you like to play it?"

Friedemann nodded, his eyes shining.

"Good. Then I shall write it down for you, and you can study it, along with the exercises."

Friedemann was very gifted, and he made rapid progress. His father was delighted, and during the lessons he often composed small works for him. Bach put together sixty-two of these in the *Little Clavier Book*. Friedemann loved these tiny masterpieces.

Soon Friedemann graduated from the *Little Clavier Book* and was hungry for something more difficult. So his father composed the *Inventions*, fifteen new, more advanced works with two- and three-part melody. Those short compositions are full of imagination and gusto.

"See, Friede dear, how one can create a whole new composition on a short theme. We shall study how this is done."

With Bach as teacher, practicing never became drudgery, and lessons were adventures for all his pupils. "I want a round, beautiful, singing tone on the keyboard," Bach told them, "as if a bow were drawn over the strings. The sounds should melt into each other. Let me show you."

He played the composition, once, twice, three times. "Do you hear? Now, you try."

The pupil taking the lesson tried to play. Bach yelled, "Sing! Make the instrument sing! Again, from the beginning."

The pupil tried again. Bach boomed, "Sing! Make the melody your own!"

What lively, inspiring lessons! No two were alike. Bach was patient but firm with beginners. Often the new pupil was frightened and said, "Please, master, give me something very, very easy to play."

"I will see what I can do for you." And Bach composed something appropriate.

The pupil tried to play and fumbled. Flushed with embarrassment, he said, "Thank you so very much, Master Bach. But this is still too difficult for me."

Bach smiled. "Practice, practice, practice. It will go very well. You have five healthy fingers on each hand just as I have."

What a wonderful time they all had at the Cöthen house! Bach, Barbara, the children, the resident students, the day pupils, and the visiting musicians all studied, practiced, composed, and played. They ate, drank, and dreamt music! The house buzzed with activity during the day. Bach composed late at night when it was quiet. He did not have to try his ideas on an instrument. He heard the music in his head and then set it down, often straining his eyes through long hours of work.

Bach's new patron, Prince Leopold, was as enthusiastic as any of the students. He and Bach were on excellent terms; he was godfather of Bach's most recent baby. Prince Leopold was a gay, charming young man of twenty-three. He loved music above all else. He sang beautifully and played several instruments.

The prince belonged to the Calvinist Protestant Church, and this meant that no elaborate music could be played in church. Therefore, Bach had at his disposal no large instrument, only a small court organ.

That left him plenty of time to create works for other instruments. As cappellmeister of the court, he could have his works performed by the eighteen musicians of the prince's orchestra. Prince Leopold played in the orchestra too, and so did Bach, conducting at the same time.

Working for such a congenial, cultured prince was a delight, and Bach composed one work after another. Among them was the romantic *Chromatic Fantasy and Fugue*.

"A fugue should touch one's heart," Bach used to say.

At that time he created the ever-popular *Italian Concerto,* several sonatas for flute and for unaccompanied cello, several violin concerti, and many other works.

He composed *Six Sonatas for Unaccompanied Violin,* works which required performers with exceptional skill. The last movement of the *Fourth Sonata for Unaccompanied Violin* (Second Partita in D Minor), the "Chaconne," has become especially famous.

The word chaconne was the name of a Spanish dance. Bach's "Chaconne" is a monumental work with a great depth of feeling. Today it is also played on other instruments, frequently the piano.

Prince Leopold had many friends throughout the countryside, and he took Bach with him when he traveled, even to Carlsbad, a resort he visited annually. There, Bach met Christian Ludwig, margrave of Brandenburg. The margrave loved music. "Please, Mr. Bach, will you compose something for my orchestra?" he asked.

An excerpt from Bach's "Chaconne" in the great
musician's own handwriting

"With pleasure, Your Highness," Bach replied.

Three years later, Bach sent the margrave *Six
Brandenburg Concerti*, with a long handwritten
dedication. In it, Bach begged the margrave "to
overlook the imperfections of the works."

Those "imperfect" works are glorious compositions with an irresistible and joyful dancing drive.
In the *Fifth Brandenburg Concerto*, Bach gave a
large solo part to the keyboard instrument. At
that time, in orchestra pieces, the keyboard instrument was rarely heard alone. Bach was the
first composer to develop the concerto for keyboard instrument.

Bach was also busy composing works for Friedemann. "Friedemann is making such progress!" he told Barbara one day.

"He works hard," Barbara remarked. "He wants to please you. He adores you so!"

Bach wrote twenty-four preludes and fugues for his son and his other pupils, in all keys of the scale. This had never been attempted before.

Bach named his new collection the *Well-Tempered Clavier*, for the compositions were to be played on keyboard instruments tuned in a new, or "well-tempered," way. Every prelude and fugue is different—some are gay, some are sad, and some are like a conversation between a man and a woman, others are robust dances or quiet confidences.

Prelude in C Major

The Prelude in C Major (the first) has been widely popularized by Gounod who, 125 years later, incorporated it in his song "Ave Maria."

Friedemann and the other pupils never tired of studying and playing those preludes and fugues. The advanced students loved them too.

Later, the great composers Beethoven and Chopin practiced the *Well-Tempered Clavier* constantly. The famous twentieth century cellist Pablo Casals always started his day by playing two preludes and fugues on the piano. No wonder that they have been called the "One Thousand and One Nights of Music."

12. A Tragic Loss

In June 1720 Bach accompanied Prince Leopold on his annual visit to Carlsbad. Bach enjoyed the trip, for he always met interesting people at this resort.

Still he missed his family. When he returned to Cöthen, he hurried home. He had so many things to tell Barbara! Eagerly he opened the door of the house. What? No music? Why so quiet? Where was everybody?

Dorothea, Friedemann, Emanuel, and Bernhard rose to meet him. They threw themselves in his arms. All of them were sobbing.

"What's the matter? What's going on here? Where is your mother? Is she sick?"

They shook their heads sadly. It was worse than sickness. Barbara had died suddenly a few days before, from an unknown disease. She was already buried. There had not been enough time to send Bach a message before he left Carlsbad.

Poor Bach! Many weeks and months passed before he could begin to recover from this terrible blow. He composed a Sonata in C Minor for clavier and violin in which the slow movement, the "Largo," speaks of his grief. This same melody he used again later in his famous *St. Matthew Passion*, in the aria for alto, "Pity O God, Because of My Tears."

In those dark days Bach felt more and more that he wanted to play again on a large organ, compose church organ music, and listen to it. He went to Prince Leopold.

"Your Highness, I have learned that the position

of organist at St. Jakob's Church in Hamburg is vacant. I want to send in my application."

"And if you are accepted, you will want to leave. Is that it? Well . . . I understand."

Bach went to Hamburg for an audition with the St. Jakob's church board. As he walked the familiar streets, he remembered how happy he had been there when he was seventeen, listening in rapture to old Master Reinken. He decided to see if he could play the organ in Reinken's church, St. Catherine.

The church board of St. Catherine agreed and announced a concert by Bach. A large audience gathered. Bach climbed to the organ loft and sat on the bench alone. All was quiet. Eighteen years before Reinken had played a dazzling composition on the chorale taken from Psalm 137, "By the Waters of Babylon We Sat and Wept." Bach recalled the glorious performance.

Now it was his turn. He pulled out the stops, steadied himself on the bench, and, beginning with the theme of the same chorale, started to play. He played with his whole soul and heart. The music sang of his bereavement and his grief.

The stupendous improvisation lasted half an hour. The people sat entranced as the music filled the church.

When Bach came down from the organ loft, the crowd was hushed. A very old man came forward —Reinken! The ninety-six-year-old master took Bach's hands in his and said, "I thought this art was long dead, but I see that it lives in you."

Many citizens of Hamburg wanted to see Bach appointed as the church organist of St. Jakob's. However, the church board gave preference to a young musician whose father was a rich merchant in Hamburg.

Bach went back to Cöthen and his motherless children. With the aid of a servant, thirteen-year-old Dorothea was doing her best to keep house and look after the younger children. But the burden was too heavy for her young shoulders. A year had passed since Barbara's untimely death. People in Cöthen began to say, "Mr. Bach is young, only thirty-six; he should remarry."

At Prince Leopold's court there was a new singer, twenty-year-old Anna Magdalena Wilke, who had an exquisite soprano voice. Bach heard her and was delighted. Anna Magdalena was relieved that her singing had pleased Cappellmeister Bach. She did not know that he also liked her looks, her quiet, unassuming ways, and her kind eyes. To her, Master Bach was an older musician, an outstanding performer, and a friend of the prince.

It came as a surprise to her when one day Master Bach asked, "Miss Wilke, will you marry me?"

Marry the master! A widower, sixteen years older than she was and with four children—thirteen, eleven, seven, and six. And what about her own career? Anna Magdalena thought of all this. However, she did not hesitate. She was a courageous, warmhearted young woman, and she admired the master greatly.

"Miss Wilke," Bach repeated, "will you marry me?"

"Yes, I will," she said.

Bach told Prince Leopold. "My dear Bach," said the prince, "this is the right thing to do. I am going to marry too."

Bach and Anna Magdalena were married quietly.

The prince kept her on as a court singer, and she continued to draw a handsome salary. Yet her outside work did not prevent her from taking full charge of Bach's home.

Anna Magdalena was gentle and patient, always ready to listen to Bach and his music, and to help him in every way. Bach came to love her very much. He wrote poems about her which he set to music. One day he brought her the following one:

> If you are near me
> Joyfully will I go
> Toward heavenly rest and peace.
> Nothing will I fear
> If I hear your lovely voice,
> And if your beautiful hands close
> my faithful eyes.

Bach's young wife was gifted musically. She wished to learn to play the clavichord. Bach composed for her some keyboard works and songs and had them bound in a green leather book with brown corners. The title was *Little Clavier Book for Anna Magdalena Bach, Year 1722.*

Anna Magdalena loved flowers as well as music. People in Cöthen admired her garden very much.

They said, "Anna Magdalena takes care of flowers as well as she takes care of the children."

Prince Leopold had also married. The princess was a pretty, merry young woman. However, she had no interest in music whatsoever. Soon she began to complain. "Leopold, you prefer Mr. Bach's company to mine!" she pouted.

The prince was eager to please her. He began to see less of Bach and to participate less in music making.

Bach was hurt. He said to Anna Magdalena, "I am not wanted here anymore. I shall have to look for a position elsewhere. Anyway, I would like to be associated with a church that has a good organ."

He heard that a cantor was needed at St. Thomas' Church in Leipzig. The cantor would also be director of music for all the Leipzig churches. "I am going to apply," Bach said.

There were two other applicants, and one of them was Telemann, Bach's long-time friend. The Leipzig council commissioned the three applicants to write a composition on a special subject. They chose the St. John Passion for Bach. He had to compose an oratorio, a sacred work for voices and instruments, on the story of Jesus' death as narrated in the Gospel according to St. John.

Bach was glad to compose for voices again. Besides, he felt inspired by the subject. He, too, had known so much sadness and grief from his childhood on; so many dear ones had departed. He wrote very dramatic music, full of emotion.

Although Bach's *St. John Passion* is played today and much admired, the oratorio was not appreciated by the Leipzig council. They chose Telemann. He decided not to accept, so the council offered the post to the second applicant, who declined for financial reasons. The only applicant

A portion of Bach's contract with the Leipzig council, including Bach's signature

left was Bach. The council was not eager to appoint him. One of the councilmen remarked, "We have no choice. Since we could not get the best, we have to be content with what is mediocre."

Mediocre! Bach! The man who is considered by many today as the greatest musical genius of all time!

Bach's acceptance of the position was hard on Anna Magdalena. She would have to leave many friends and a pleasant job. St. Thomas' Church did not allow women singers.

Bach tried to explain why he felt the move was important. "You see, dear, in a cultural center such as Leipzig, we shall be able to give the boys a better education. The children will have what I wanted and could not have—a university education."

In May 1723 Bach and his family said good-bye to Cöthen where he had been so immensely happy and so profoundly distressed. There he had composed much of his most beautiful instrumental music.

13. Twenty Children

"Dinner is ready," announced Dorothea, now a young lady of twenty. The Bachs gathered around the big table. They had been living in Leipzig for five years, and forty-three-year-old Johann Sebastian and Anna Magdalena had two children of their own, four-year-old Heinrich and two-year-old Elisabeth, as well as Barbara's three boys and a girl.

"Let me tell you a story," Bach said to the younger children. "You are going to meet a lot of cousins later this year, as it is our turn to play host at the yearly Bach gathering. So you need to learn some of the family history. Do you know that Bachs have been musicians for many generations, even Great-Great-Grandfather Viet Bach, the miller?"

"The miller?" asked Heinrich.

"He was a miller *and* a musician. He played the zither to the accompaniment of his mill wheel."

"Zum! Zum!" sang Bernhard, now thirteen, turning an imaginary wheel with his hand. Bach smiled and went on, "Viet's son, Hans, was a carpet weaver, and he played the violin. Hans the Fiddler, as he was called, was very popular, especially at weddings. One of his sons was my grandfather. He was a violinist and an organist, the first Bach to make music his profession. His son, my father, was, as you know, the town musician at Eisenach."

"I wish we had known Grandfather Ambrosius," remarked fourteen-year-old Emanuel.

"I wish you had. My father was so kind and gay! . . . But you still have plenty of relatives."

"All those uncles and great-uncles, and cousins, all musicians," put in Friedemann.

"And there are new ones born every year," Bach laughed.

The church of St. Thomas and adjoining school
faced a spacious square in busy Leipzig.

"I am grateful," said Anna Magdalena, "that this house is so large. As it is, I still don't know where we will put them all when they come to visit."

The Bachs' rambling living quarters were part of a wing of Leipzig's St. Thomas' School. The building, which was next to St. Thomas' Church, was old and uncomfortable. Bach's home was separated from the school proper by only a thin partition. All day long the Bachs could hear the singsong of the school children repeating their lessons. Bach composed at night, when it was quiet, in his study on the second floor.

The city of Leipzig was large for the time and had 30,000 inhabitants. Besides its university, Leipzig had an opera house and a theater. Friedemann was about to enter the university to study law, philosophy, and mathematics. Two years later, Emanuel would follow. This was a source of deep satisfaction to Bach and helped counteract the many difficulties he experienced in Leipzig.

At Cöthen Bach had had one employer; at Leipzig he had three: the town council, the school board, and the church board. The three employers did not agree on the policy regarding the "cantor" of St. Thomas'. Bach himself considered that his most important title was director of music for the Leipzig churches. That's what interested him.

Soon after his arrival he had arranged for someone else to assume the cantor's duty of teaching Latin at the school. No one had objected. But he still was expected to direct the choir boys and to teach them music and catechism. In addition, he was in charge of school discipline one day every fourth week.

On that day, Bach had to be at school when the pupils got up—4 A.M. in summer, 5 A.M. in winter. All day, until 8 P.M., he was responsible for the boys' good behavior. The pupils were dirty, ill-fed, often rude and rebellious. Bach was at a loss as to how to control them.

The day was a nightmare to him. He was relieved when it was over and he could resume his music. He wrote a new cantata for the Sunday service every week.

In his Leipzig cantatas, Bach sang of death and resurrection as in "Christ in Death's Bonds," of battle and victory as in "A Mighty Fortress," based on Luther's chorale. He told of humble, homely, everyday occurrences in "Sleep My Love," part of his *Christmas Oratorio.*

Bach also created powerful instrumental compositions such as the Prelude and Fugue in B Minor (the "Great").

Every week the choir boys and the orchestra players had to have copies of the new work. Anna Magdalena copied the music by hand. Sometimes she got the older children to help her.

Even morning prayers were an occasion for making music in the lively Bach household.

Bach adored children. He and Barbara had had seven. Anna Magdalena eventually had thirteen. Twenty children in all! Many of them died in infancy, however, as was not uncommon then when medical knowledge was limited. He and Anna Magdalena knew grief many times, but they did not let it darken the days for the youngsters still alive. Bach expected the children to be hard-working and God-fearing; however, he wanted them to have a good time too. Their home was lively and gay, especially during fair time.

The Leipzig International Fair was famous. It was devoted to books and attracted many visitors.

Anna Magdalena took the younger children to the entertainment booths at the fair. Coming home from work, Bach was met by a deafening din of toy drums, paper horns, and whirligigs.

"Papa," they cried, "we saw clowns and freaks, and animals doing tricks!"

"What did the animals do?" he asked. Before the children could answer, he was on all fours running around the room and roaring. The children scattered in every direction, shrieking and laughing. Such good times they had with their father!

14. Quarrels

If only things had gone as well for Bach at church as at home. He was continually having difficulty with the church board and the town council.

Bach was particularly exasperated with the university board. They looked down on him because he did not have a university degree. On his arrival, they told him they did not want him to be director of music at the university church.

"I was hired as director of music for all the Leipzig churches," Bach told them.

However, the university had temporarily appointed Johann Gottlieb Görner as their music director. Görner, who was much younger than

Bach, was also the organist at St. Nicholas', one of the Leipzig churches.

Bach was angry. The loss of the university position lessened his prestige. If only Görner had been a good musician, he would not have minded so much.

One day as Bach was directing a rehearsal at St. Nicholas', Görner, who was at the organ, hit so many wrong notes that Bach became exasperated. He snatched his own wig and flung it at Görner's head, shouting, "You ought to have been a cobbler!" Yet this "cobbler" was the man to whom the university had bestowed the title of director of music to the university!

Bach wrote to the king, appealing the university's decision. The king tried to please everybody —the university kept Görner as their year-round director of music, and Bach was named director of music for the university church festivals.

Bach also had difficulties with the parishioners at St. Thomas' Church. The people of Leipzig did not understand or appreciate many of Bach's compositions.

On Easter Sunday, in 1729, Bach went to St.

Thomas' Church before dawn. The Easter service began at 7 A.M. and lasted until noon. It was a chilly day and people hurried to church carrying foot-warmer boxes filled with red-hot coals.

Bach sat at the organ, playing and directing his new work, the *St. Matthew Passion*. Bach was in full command of his singers and forty orchestra players, while at the same time he played on both organ keyboards with his hands, and on the pedal keyboard with his feet moving at top speed.

The incredibly beautiful music of the *St. Matthew Passion* filled the church. Its novelty distracted and shocked the faithful. Bach made use of St. Thomas' unusual facilities: two organs and two balconies about fifty feet apart. He had two orchestras and two choirs answering each other. Sometimes the music was heard from the left, sometimes from the right, sometimes both.

People looked at one another and whispered, "What is this?" It was not their idea of religious music. "God save us, my children!" exclaimed an old lady. "This is an opera!"

After the service, complaints began to pour in to the church board, and Bach was scolded.

Johann Sebastian Bach at the organ

"Living in Leipzig is too aggravating," Bach told Anna Magdalena.

Anna Magdalena did her best to make life pleasant for him, and Bach himself tried to be content. He had so many plans in mind for the music in the churches.

"I'm going to ask the town council for more choir boys and more orchestra players," he told Anna Magdalena one morning. "I need more people if my cantatas and larger works, such as the *Magnificat*, are to be performed properly."

"How wonderful it will be if the council agrees!" Anna Magdalena said.

But the council refused to grant Bach's request. What was worse, it admitted to the school many boys Bach had rejected as being totally unmusical.

Soon the performances at St. Thomas' Church deteriorated. The council accused Bach of not giving the boys enough of his time.

One day, Bach came home furious. "Do you know, Anna Magdalena, what happened? The council has decided to reduce my salary because I am 'incorrigible.' That's their own word! I tell you it is high time that we move on. I am

118

going to write my old school friend Erdmann, who is now working in Danzig, and ask him to find me another post."

However, Erdmann could not find a suitable position for Bach.

Forced to remain in Leipzig, Bach depended more than ever on his family for happiness. Their concerts were a great joy to him. All the children were fine musicians and singers. Bach composed all sorts of works for his family to play, such as the exciting Concerto in D Minor and the simpler Fantasy in C Minor.

Resident students living with the Bachs joined in the family concerts too. Moreover, there was always a new baby. Often Bach had to pick up a crawling child curious about the movement of the harpsichord pedals.

But even the happiness at home could not compensate for the pettiness and wrangling Bach had to endure from the town council, the school board, and the church board.

15. Coffee and Tarts

One fall day in 1730, Bach came home radiant. "Johann Matthias Gessner has been made director of the St. Thomas' School!"

"Ah," said Anna Magdalena, "I am so glad! He was such a good friend when you were in Weimar."

Happy days returned, and with them inspiration. Bach composed a great many pieces of chamber music, some new *suites,* and also *overtures* for orchestra. The first D Major Overture is particularly famous. A century later, the great violinist Paganini played part of the composition on one string. From then on it became the well-known "Aria for G String."

Bach also composed for King August III. The king was a Catholic, and he asked Bach to compose a mass for him. Thus Bach became the first and only Protestant composer to write a mass for the Catholic church. The genius of the *Mass in B Minor* defies description. It is a composition of sublime grandeur and heartrending tenderness, considered by some to be the greatest musical work ever created. Because it requires so many performers, it is played mostly in concert halls and not in church.

Ag - nus De - - i qui tol - - lis pecca - - ta mun - di

As a reward, the king gave Bach the title of court composer. Bach was proud of this honorary title.

Even the university began to appreciate him, though mostly as a performer. Bach had been appointed permanent director of the Collegium Musicum several years before. This was a university students' ensemble, which Georg Philipp

Telemann had founded when he himself was a student in Leipzig. The students met once a week, played at official festivities, and gave concerts the year around. Bach enjoyed working with these young people immensely, and the concerts became popular.

During the summer the group often performed at Zimmermann's Coffee House. Anna Magdalena and the children would accompany Bach to the café.

It was so pleasant sitting at the tables in Zimmermann's garden. Leipzig families, out-of-town business people, and crowds from the fair gathered there to relax under the trees, to drink, eat, and enjoy music. Zimmermann's tarts were famous and, besides wine and beer, he served the new drink—coffee.

Coffee had been introduced in France by the Turkish ambassador and had soon become very fashionable all over Europe. Ladies in Leipzig had to drink it; it was the thing to do.

"Who wants another piece of tart?" Anna Magdalena asked one afternoon at Zimmermann's.

"I! I!" shrieked all the children.

"All right. We shall all have some as soon as Gottfried Reiche has played his trumpet solo. You know, papa composed this serenade especially for him."

When the serenade ended, people called, " 'The Coffee Cantata'! Mr. Bach! 'The Coffee Cantata'!"

Bach nodded gaily. He began regrouping his musicians and singers. Meanwhile Zimmermann came around with a large tray of tarts. The children were delighted. Coffee was served to the adults.

"This is the right time to drink coffee!" said Zimmermann with a wink.

Bach had composed a cantata about the new drink. "The Coffee Cantata" was like a merry, tiny opera. A young girl, Lisbeth, likes coffee. She sings its praise:

Ah! What a treat coffee is!

But her father disapproves of the new drink. He tells her that he will not find her a husband unless she gives up coffee. Lisbeth obeys, and her father finds her a suitable young man. Lisbeth likes the young man and tells him she will marry

him, provided he promises, and has it written in
the marriage contract:

> That she shall always, at command,
> Have coffee whenever she pleases.

The young man agrees, and the cantata ends with
the two singing:

> Cats must have mice,
> And young women coffee!

People in the garden joined in the singing. What
fun they had! Bach himself enjoyed these informal
open-air concerts, and so did his pupils.

All Bach's pupils were devoted to him. As one
of them used to say, "The master transforms hours
into minutes." The pupils were also greatly attached to Anna Magdalena, whom they called "the
most lovable mamma." She looked after everybody
and was an intimate part of her husband's musical
life.

16. Bach's Pupils Come of Age

While Bach's friend, Gessner, was director of St. Thomas' School, life was pleasant for the Bachs at Leipzig. Unfortunately, when he left after four years, he was replaced by an autocratic man who did not care for music.

One Sunday, Bach climbed to the organ loft where the choir had assembled. He found in charge not his regular assistant or prefect, but a young man named Krause. The director had appointed him prefect without telling Bach.

"Out you go!" Bach angrily told Krause. Then he motioned to his regular prefect to take charge.

The service began. Suddenly footsteps were heard on the stairway, and the director appeared followed by Krause. Krause, backed by the director, attempted to throw Bach's prefect downstairs. Bach was indignant and protested loudly. The director tried to outshout him. "Choir boys," the director barked, "if you do not obey Krause, I shall withhold your salaries." The quarrel could be heard throughout the entire church.

Soon the whole town spoke of nothing else. Every Sunday there was the same row again. Finally Bach took to directing the choir himself.

Bach directing the choir at St. Thomas' Church

The situation was so bad that he and Anna Magdalena began to worry about the future of their children, should Bach be forced to leave Leipzig. "It is wiser for Bernhard to secure a position right away instead of going to the university," Bach said to Anna Magdalena. "I can arrange for him to be accepted at Mülhausen as organist."

"You know, Johann Sebastian, that he wants to go to the university."

"I know. But, unfortunately, conditions here are too uncertain. It is best that he starts out on his own now."

Bernhard was disappointed, but he went to Mülhausen. Soon he was in trouble there—he began to squander his money.

Bach learned what was happening and was deeply upset. He settled with Bernhard's creditors, but soon afterwards Bernhard disappeared. For months his anxious parents did not know where he was. At last they heard that he was in Jena, studying law and supporting himself by helping his elderly cousin Nicholas. Then four months later, the gifted and reckless Bernhard died suddenly. He was only twenty-four. What a blow to his father and stepmother!

It was comforting to know that at least "Friede dear" was doing well as organist at the Dresden court.

Emanuel was also a credit to his parents. He had his university degree and was about to enter the services of Frederick the Great, king of Prussia, as a harpsichordist. Bach was pleased, though Berlin seemed faraway to him. Bach, now fifty-five, was begining to have serious trouble with his eyesight, and he liked to have his family near. Since childhood, he had strained his eyes copying music in poor light.

He was full of energy, however, and still had many children to bring up. Baby Carolina was only three. Christian, aged five, and Christoph, aged eight, were both very musical. Fourteen-year-old Elisabeth was gifted too. But Heinrich had never developed mentally. Gentle and dearly loved by all, he had to be looked after at sixteen as if he were still a little boy. Patient Dorothea, still unmarried, helped with all the children. In 1742 the Bachs' last child, Susanna, was born.

The busy household always included resident students, as Bach was increasingly popular as a teacher. Johann Theophilus Goldberg, a brilliant harpsichordist, lived with the Bachs for several years. When he left, he became the personal musician of Count Keyserling, who admired Bach greatly.

Soon, young Goldberg had a problem. Count Keyserling, who loved music, could not sleep. All through the night he kept saying, "Play, my dear Goldberg, play!" Exhausted, Goldberg went on playing. But the restless count was not satisfied with Goldberg's repertoire. He wanted something new and soothing to put him to sleep.

Finally one day he said, "I know what to do, my dear Goldberg. I am going to ask the master to compose some pleasing variations that you can play for me."

Bach wrote an astonishing set of thirty variations for the count, covering all styles of music, from majestic to popular tunes. Count Keyserling was pleased and sent Bach a magnificent solid gold cup filled with gold coins.

From then on, whenever he could not sleep, the

count would say, "My dear Goldberg, play *my* variations." These variations were complex and difficult, and Goldberg had to work hard. There was no sleep for him! But at least his patron was satisfied. In time the composition became known as the *Goldberg Variations.* They are frequently played today in concerts.

Two years after composing the *Goldberg Variations,* Bach finished the second volume of the *Well-Tempered Clavier.* Its twenty-four preludes and fugues still inspire music students and artists the world over.

In 1745 war broke out between Prussia and Austria. Frederick the Great of Prussia was on the march. His armies were advancing through the German states.

Bach hated war, and he was deeply distressed. To express his feelings, he composed a cantata, "O Prince of Peace, Lord Jesus." When the armies neared Leipzig, he became concerned for his household, but the war soon ended in victory for Prussia, and Leipzig was safe.

Now the Bachs worried about Emanuel, who was in Berlin in the service of King Frederick.

Weeks and months went by without word from him. At long last, two years later, a letter came. "It's from Emanuel!" Anna Magdalena announced joyfully.

Bach, now sixty years old, found reading more and more difficult, so Anna Magdalena opened the letter. "Johann Sebastian!" she cried excitedly, "we are grandparents! Emanuel has married, and he has two children—a boy and a girl!"

"A boy and a girl! I wish we could see them!"

"You can, Johann Sebastian." She went on reading. "Emanuel writes that King Frederick would like you to visit him and play for him. The king is musical and admires you greatly."

17. "Old Bach Is Here"

Emanuel met the coach in Berlin, together with Friedemann who had come from Dresden to visit.

Bach stepped down from the coach, his suit dusty and rumpled. The journey from Leipzig had been hard but he smiled happily, his fatigue forgotten when he saw his sons.

"Papa!" cried Emanuel, "the king wants to see you at once!"

"I'll be ready, as soon as I have changed my suit and kissed my grandchildren."

"Papa," said Friedemann, "Emanuel means that you have to go straight to the palace, just as you are. That's what the king said."

Bach frowned. Then he looked at his eager sons, shrugged his shoulders, and followed them.

As they entered the palace, King Frederick, surrounded by beautifully dressed courtiers, was playing the flute. Seeing Bach he stopped at once and called joyously, "Ladies and gentlemen, old Bach is here!" Then he rushed to greet him.

"Your Majesty . . . I don't know how to apologize . . . my appearance . . ."

"It does not matter a bit, not a bit! Come with me. I want you to try my instruments—all of them—especially the first pianoforte, built by Silbermann."

The king and Bach walked through the magnificent palace rooms, followed by a crowd of noblemen and ladies. There were keyboard instruments everywhere. Bach tried all of them and improvised freely. Each time the king was more astonished at Bach's ability, as were his courtiers. They had always admired the king's musical talent, but apparently "old Bach" surpassed the king himself.

The king felt a little jealous and, suddenly, he took his flute and played a theme, a rather clumsy one. Then he said, "Mr. Bach, let us hear a fugue built on that theme."

At once Bach improvised a three-voice fugue. The noblemen and ladies were filled with admiration. But the king was the king; it was important to him to appear cleverer than his guest.

"Fine, fine, Mr. Bach," he said. "Now, what about a six-voice fugue on that theme?"

Emanuel and Friedemann looked at each other in dismay. Didn't the king know that his theme did not lend itself to such an improvisation? Was the king trying to embarrass their father? How could Bach not lose face and at the same time not offend the king?

Bach bowed to the king and said quietly, "Your Majesty, such a royal theme has to be treated as it deserves; it demands some preparation. If Your Majesty allows me, I will think about it when I am back home and will submit to Your Majesty a work truly worthy of his musicianship."

Frederick the Great opened his mouth . . . but already Bach had launched into a brilliant six-voice fugue improvisation on a theme of his own. Emanuel and Friedemann smiled.

Back in Leipzig Bach made good his promise to the king. *The Musical Offering* is a large composition in which Bach multiplied the technical difficulties, the scholarly developments, the acrobatic stunts, anything and everything that could utterly dazzle King Frederick. Emanuel and Friedemann enjoyed the "musical vengeance" of their father. As for Frederick the Great, he was smart enough to be aware of Bach's intention, and clever enough, also, to be amused.

Around that time, Johann Christoph Altnikol, one of Bach's resident students, came to his beloved teacher and said, "Master, may I ask you for your daughter Elisabeth's hand in marriage?"

"Christoph, I gladly give it to you."

Elisabeth loved Altnikol, and the wedding date was soon set.

Bach told Anna Magdalena, "I am going to present them with an unexpected gift. Altnikol needs work. I shall write the Naumburg Council and recommend him as organist."

Altnikol was accepted, and he and Elisabeth moved to Naumburg. It was near enough to Leipzig, so they could visit their parents often.

This was fortunate, as it meant they could still help Bach copy his music. His failing eyesight made writing more and more difficult for him.

However, the master was still busy working on his great work, *The Art of the Fugue*. He wanted to show all that can possibly be done with a musical theme in the fugue form. He tried to sum up all he knew and had experienced about composing during his lifetime. Bach introduced his own name in the music, giving each letter the sound it has in German: B (b flat), A (a), C (c), H (b natural).

The Art of the Fugue is the last composition in Bach's own handwriting. Before long he could hardly see at all, and he began to dictate his music to Altnikol.

People in Leipzig began talking about Bach's failing health. The council was concerned and decided to look for a successor at once. Bach was indignant. "I am not dead yet!" he roared. He fought the council so determinedly that the successor had to leave town.

However, Bach's sight kept deteriorating and with it the general state of his health. "I shall have my eyes operated on," he said. "I have heard of an English surgeon who does marvels."

He had two operations—in March and in April 1750. He suffered a great deal, but the painful operations were a failure. He became totally blind and ran a high fever. Soon he had to be confined to bed completely.

Anna Magdalena sat by his bedside day and night. One evening Bach said to her, "Beloved, you must be so tired. Go to bed."

"Yes, please, mama," said Altnikol. "I will take the night watch."

It was so quiet in the room, Altnikol thought Bach had gone to sleep. All of a sudden he sat up and called, "Christoph, get some writing paper. I want to dictate some music."

He dictated a chorale, "Before Thy Throne Herewith I Stand." "Christoph," he said as he finished dictating, "this is my last composition in this world."

Early one morning not long afterwards, he called eagerly, "Anna Magdalena!" She rushed to his bedside. He was sitting up, and his eyes were open. "I can see! I can see you!" And for a few minutes he could see. Then suddenly he fell back on his pillow, exhausted. He was blind again.

His eyesight never returned. He grew worse and worse. On July 28, 1750, he asked, "Make some music, Anna Magdalena." Her hand in his, she began to sing the chorale, "All Men Have to Die." Everyone present joined in singing the various parts. A great calm spread over Bach's face, and he died quietly. He was sixty-five years old.

For about 100 years, Bach's genius as a composer was not recognized, and his works were ignored. Mozart (1756–1791) was deeply impressed by the grandeur of Bach's compositions; however, his interest could not prevent Bach's music from falling into oblivion. At that time, it was the custom for each organist to compose and play his own music, so Bach's compositions were not performed.

People remembered Bach, but they thought of him as a brilliant musical performer, especially on the organ, and as a fine teacher, rather than as a great composer. His works had been considered inflated, artificial, and confusing, even in his lifetime. People preferred the compositions of his

Two of Bach's gifted sons: Johann Christian (left) and Wilhelm Friedemann (right)

gifted sons, Wilhelm Friedemann, Carl Philipp Emanuel, and Johann Christian Bach.

Then, around 1830, the famous composer Mendelssohn discovered the *St. Matthew Passion* and the *Passacaglia*. He recognized immediately the greatness and the beauty of Bach's music. His enthusiasm had no limits. Under his leadership the *St. Matthew Passion* was performed in the St. Thomas' Church in Leipzig.

From then on, Bach the composer began to be appreciated, first by professional musicians, then by the general public. The Bach Society was founded. The manuscripts that still existed—a great many were lost—were printed and reprinted. People began to feel the beauty, universality, and uniqueness of Bach's music and to consider him the greatest composer Europe had ever known. His use of many voices and instruments to weave various melodies together was beyond compare and opened the way for new music to come.

It is no longer necessary to be a churchgoer to hear Bach's music. It is played everywhere—in homes, in concert halls, on the radio and television, and on all kinds of instruments. Some composers have even adapted Bach's themes to jazz and rock rhythms.

Over 200 years after his death, Bach speaks to us directly; he asks questions, he comforts, he calls, he challenges us. He is a poet, a painter, and an architect in music.

Johann Sebastian Bach has something to say to everyone: in time of grief, in happiness, in loneliness, and in collective joy. His music expresses our most important experiences—life, death, love.

Music giant "old Bach is here," forever young.

Glossary

aria—an elaborate song or melody, which is part of an opera, oratorio, or cantata, for solo voice (occasionally a duet) with instrumental accompaniment

cantata—a short, dramatic musical production which may be secular or religious, written for several solo singers, chorus, organ, and a small orchestra

capriccio—a light, whimsical musical composition

chorale—a hymn of the German Protestant Church, sung to a traditional melody

clavichord—a keyboard instrument where the tone is produced by tiny brass blades striking the strings

clavier—a stringed instrument with a keyboard, like a piano

concerto—a musical composition for one or more solo instruments accompanied by an orchestra

counterpoint—a musical technic of composition where related but independent melodies can be heard separately

fantasy (or *fantasia*)—a musical composition in free form

fugue—a musical composition into which singers or instruments enter successively, imitating the main theme in various ways

harpsichord—an instrument with one or more keyboards, the tone of which is produced by a quill plucking the string when the key is depressed

oratorio—a large-scale musical work, usually dealing with a biblical subject and performed by a narrator, soloists, chorus, and orchestra

passacaglia—a musical composition based on a Spanish dance

passion—an oratorio which tells the story of Easter according to any one of the Four Gospels

prelude—a musical composition in free form often preceding a fugue

toccata—a brilliant instrumental composition that shows off the skill of the performer

Index

142

143